Silly Riddles

Zany School Riddles

by A. J. Sautter

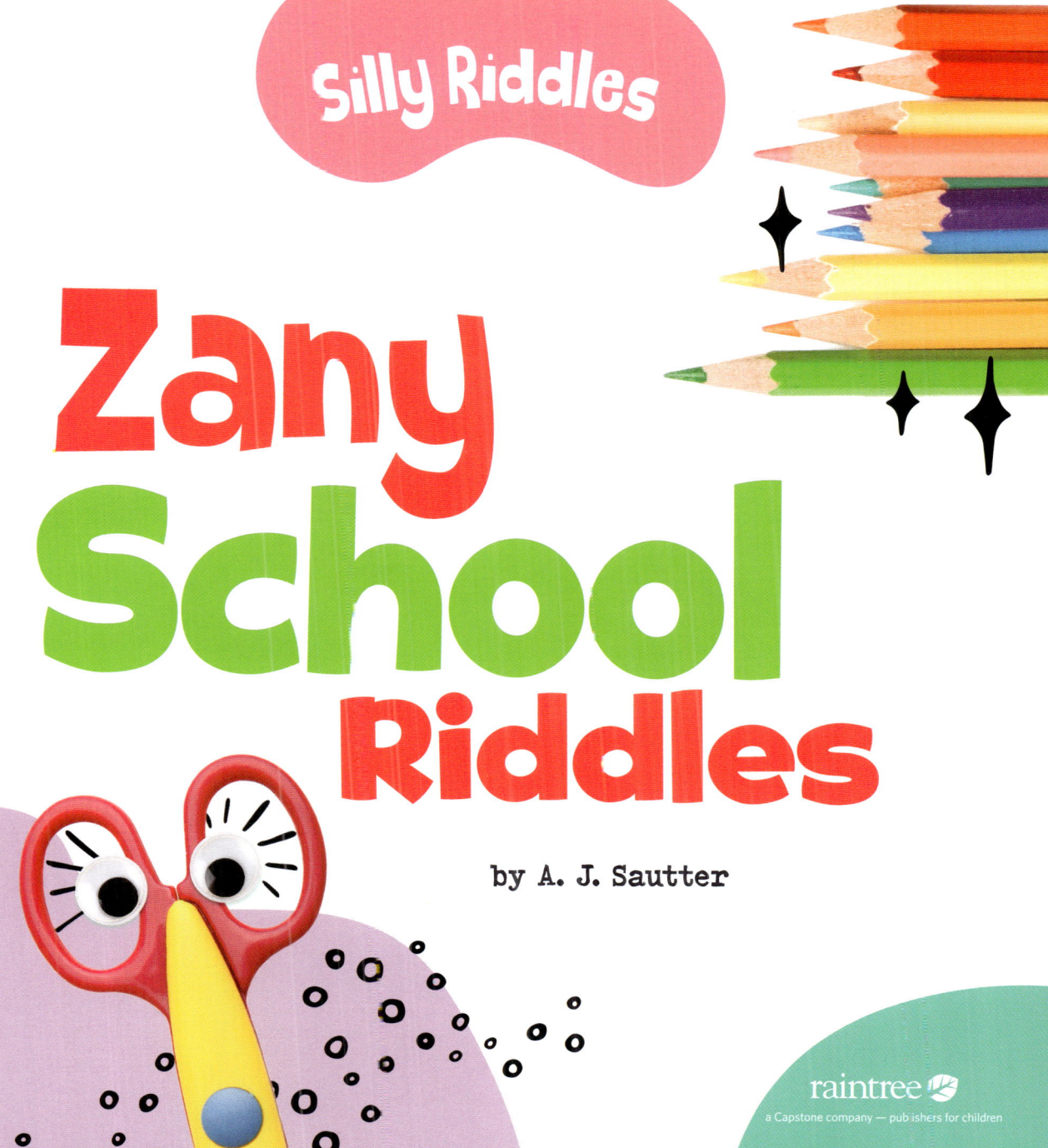

raintree
a Capstone company — pub ishers for children

Raintree is an imprint of Capstone Global Library Limited, a company incorporated in England and Wales having its registered office at 264 Banbury Road, Oxford, OX2 7DY – Registered company number: 6695582

www.raintree.co.uk
myorders@raintree.co.uk

Hardback edition text © Capstone Global Library Limited 2024
Paperback edition text © Capstone Global Library Limited 2025

The moral rights of the proprietor have been asserted. All rights reserved. No part of this publication may be reproduced in any form or by any means (including photocopying or storing it in any medium by electronic means and whether or not transiently or incidentally to some other use of this publication) without the written permission of the copyright owner, except in accordance with the provisions of the Copyright, Designs and Patents Act 1988 or under the terms of a licence issued by the Copyright Licensing Agency, 5th Floor, Shackleton House, 4 Battle Bridge Lane, London, SE1 2HX (www.cla.co.uk). Applications for the copyright owner's written permission should be addressed to the publisher.

ISBN 978 1 3982 5410 7 (hardback)
ISBN 978 1 3982 5415 2 (paperback)

Editorial Credits
Editor: Aaron Sautter; Designer: Jaime Willems; Media Researcher: Rebekah Hubstenberger; Production Specialist: Whitney Schaefer

Photo Credits
Shutterstock: anek.soowannaphoom, 18 (playground), Art789, 9 (bottom), badahos, 12 (dictionary), colnihko, design element (colour eye), creaPicTures, 19 (stamps), Daniel Prudek, 12 (bee), Dionisvera, 11 (apple), 16 (apple), eurobanks, 7 (chalkboard), Hedzun Vasyl, 8 (dinosaur), Hurst Photo, 20 (globe), Jiri Hera, 5 (coin), Kitch Bain, 15 (clock), Krakenimages.com, 21 (shoes), LittleMiss, 9 (shoes), macro videography, 17 (container), Mdesignstudio, 17 (state outline), NATALIA61, design element (googly eye), New Africa, 6 (dolphin), object_photo, 4 (gnome), oksanka007, design element (paper cutouts), Perfectorius, design element (symbols), photka, 14 (pencils), photosync, 13 (calendar), Pixel-Shot, 16 (pie), Sarkar Nataliia, cover (paper clips, coloured pencils), 1 (coloured pencils), StockArtRoom, design element (shapes), Stocksnapper, 11 (ladder), Studio KIWI, cover (scissors, ruler), 1 (scissors), 10 (triangle ruler),SvetikovaV, 21 (calendar), zhengzaishuru, 5 (octopus)

British Library Cataloguing in Publication Data
A full catalogue record for this book is available from the British Library.

Printed and bound in India.

Contents

Silly school stumpers	4
Playground puzzlers	10
Boggling brain-busters	16
Glossary	22
Find out more	23
Index	24
About the author	24

Words in **bold** are in the glossary.

Silly school stumpers

1. What did the elf do when he got home from school?

Answers!

1. He did his gnomework.

2. If Henry VIII were still alive today, what would he be most famous for?

3. What did the teacher say when Otto the octopus spoke out of turn?

Answers!

2. His age.
3. "Otto, please raise your hand, hand, hand, hand, hand, hand, hand, hand."

4. What was the first thing the young dolphin learned at school?

Answers!

4. She learned her A, B, Seas.

5. Which building in town has the most storeys?

6. What is black when it's clean and white when it's dirty?

Answers!

5. The library.
6. A chalkboard.

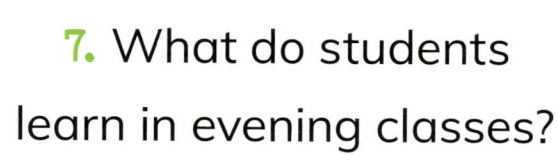

7. What do students learn in evening classes?

8. What is more impressive than a talking dinosaur?

Answers!

7. How to read in the dark.
8. A spelling bee.

9. Why is 2 + 2 = 5 just like your left foot?

10. How do young fireflies learn to do maths?

Answers!

9. Because it's not right. 10. With flash cards.

Playground puzzlers

11. What **geometric** figure is always correct?

Answers!

11. A right angle.

12. What do you get more of in **sorrow** than in anger?

13. A caretaker fell off a 6-metre ladder but didn't get hurt. Why?

Answers!

12. The letter "R".

13. He was on the bottom step.

14. Which word in the dictionary is always spelt wrong?

15. What should you do if you get a B in your maths test?

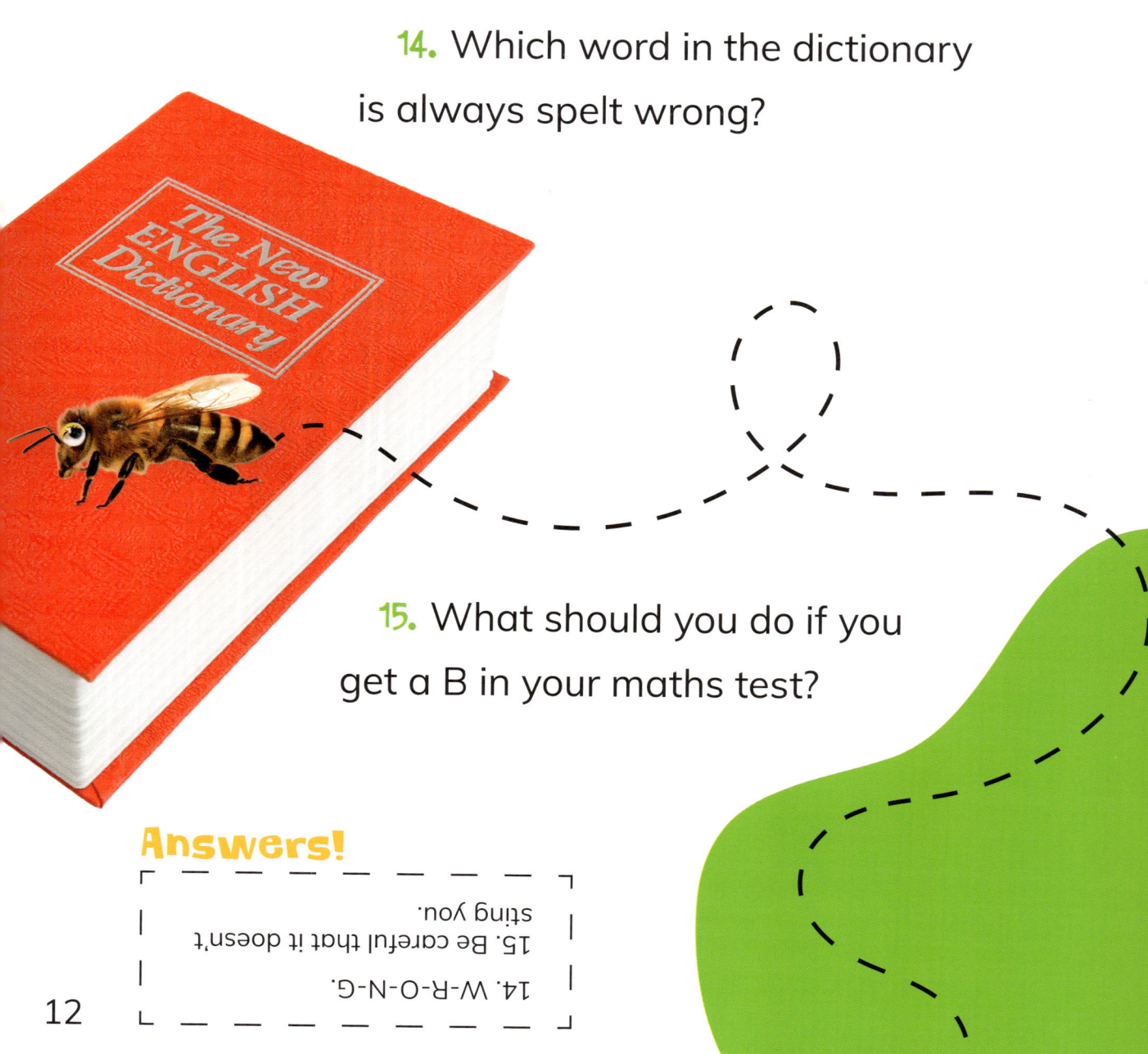

Answers!

14. W-R-O-N-G.

15. Be careful that it doesn't sting you.

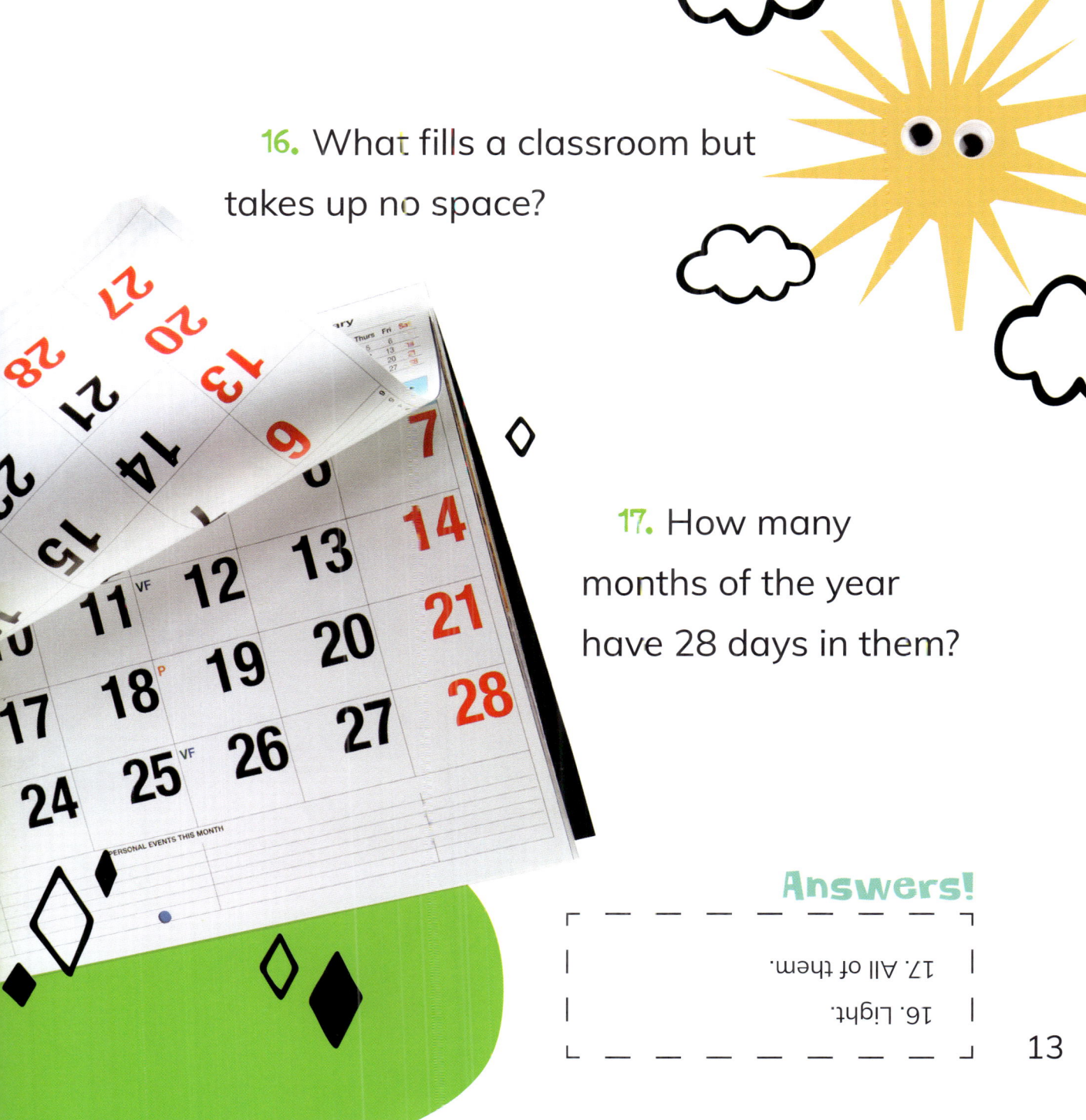

16. What fills a classroom but takes up no space?

17. How many months of the year have 28 days in them?

Answers!

16. Light.
17. All of them.

18. When does Thursday come after Friday?

19. What five-letter word becomes shorter by adding two letters to it?

Answers!
18. In the dictionary.
19. Short. Just add "ER".

20. I have no legs, but I'm always running. What am I?

Answers!

20. A clock.

Boggling brain-busters

21. A school canteen invented its own **method** for pricing food. Pie costs £3. An apple costs £5. Chocolate costs £9. How much do chips cost?

Answers!

21. Chips cost £5. The cost is £1 for each letter in the name.

22. Which US state is the most clever?

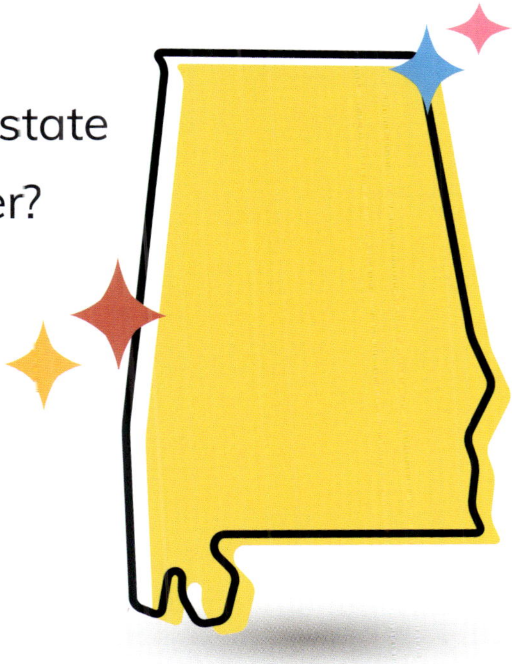

23. A container filled with water weighs 227 kilograms. What can you add to the container to make it weigh less?

Answers!

22. Alabama. It has four As and one B.
23. A hole.

24. Jada and Chloe are on the school playground. How can Jada stand behind Chloe while Chloe stands behind Jada?

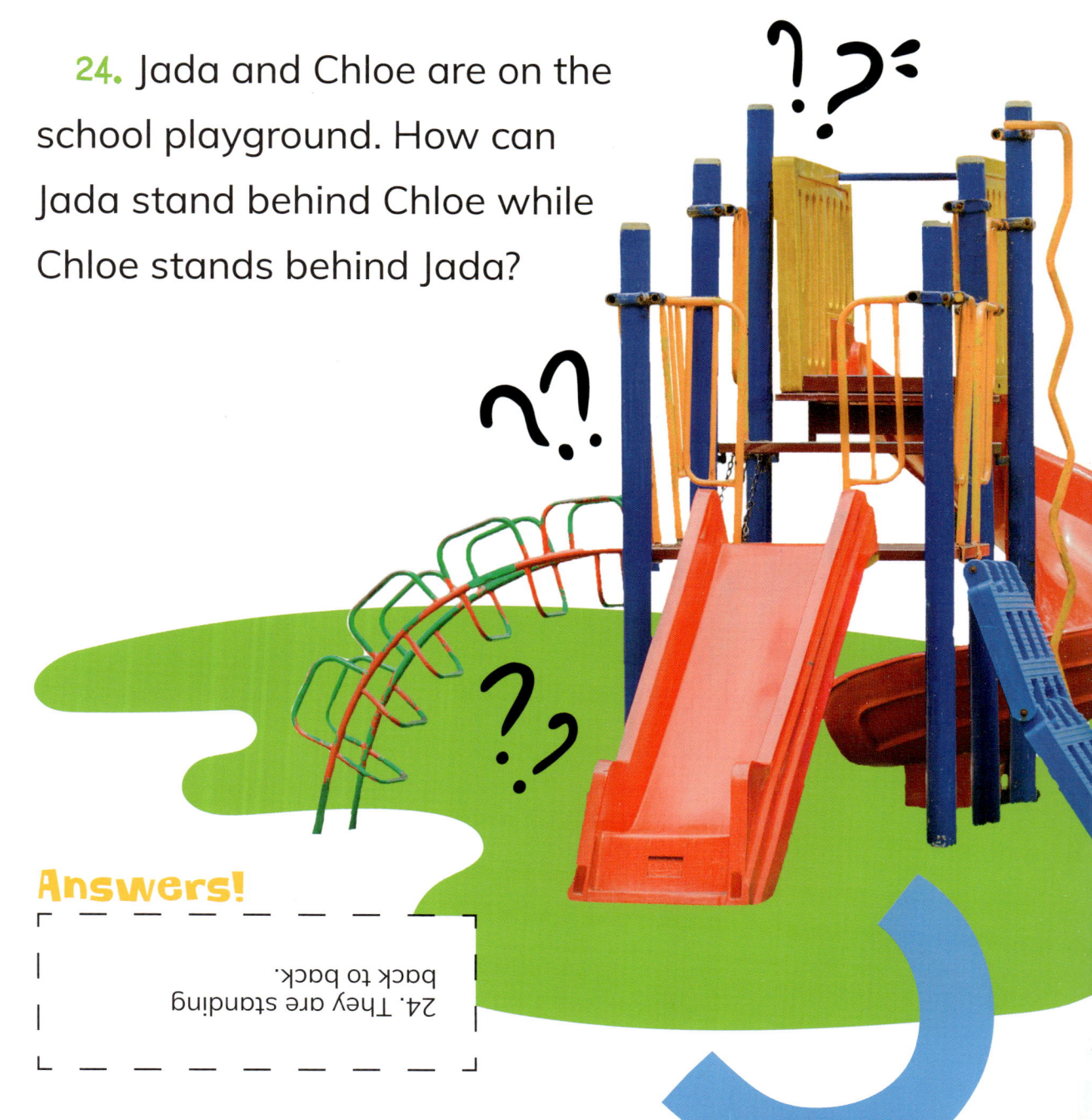

Answers!

24. They are standing back to back.

25. It takes 12 10p stamps to make a **doze**n. How many 50p stamps does it take to make a dozen?

26. Three days in a row don't appear on a calendar. What are they?

Answers!

25. 12 stamps.

26. Yesterday, today and tomorrow.

27. This has keys, but no locks. It has space, but no room. You can enter but can't go inside. What is it?

28. What has oceans without water, **forests** but no trees and cities with no roads?

Answers!

27. A computer keyboard.
28. A globe.

29. What is found once in June, three times in December, but never in July?

30. What runs around all day at school, and then lies on the floor with tongues hanging out?

Answers!

29. The letter "E".
30. Your shoes.

Glossary

dozen a group of 12

forest a large area thickly covered with trees and plants

geometric a term in maths involving points, lines and angles

method a way of doing things

sorrow a feeling of loss, sadness or regret

# Find out more

 ## Books

How to Be the Funniest Kid in School, Ivor Baddiel (Award Publications, 2023)

The Kids' Book of Awesome Riddles, Amanda Learmonth (Buster Books, 2019)

 ## Websites

50 Fantastic Riddles for Kids
letsroam.com/explorer/riddles-for-kids/

77 Awesome Riddles for Kids
prodigygame.com/main-en/blog/riddles-for-kids/

203 Fun Riddles for Kids
icebreakerideas.com/riddles-for-kids/

Index

animals 5, 6, 9

canteens 16
calendars 19
caretakers 11
chalkboards 7
classrooms 13
clocks 15

days 13, 14, 19
dinosaurs 8

elves 4

globes 20

Henry VIII 5

keyboards 20

libraries 7

maths 9, 10, 12
months 13, 21

playgrounds 18

shoes 21
stamps 19
states 17

weight 17
words 11, 12, 14

About the author

A. J. Sautter is an author and editor of dozens of kids' books on everything from aliens to zombies. He enjoys reading, going to the cinema and going for long walks with his fluffy, adorable dogs.